D1176183

WEEKLY READER BOOKS presents

What Is a Rainbow?

A **Just Ask**™ Book

Hi, my name is Christopher!

by Chris Arvetis
and Carole Palmer

illustrated by
James Buckley

FIELD PUBLICATIONS
MIDDLETOWN, CT.

Well, let me
show you.

As the sun's rays
shine through the prism,
the light is bent.
As the light bends,
it splits into many colors.

In the sunlight
there are many colors.

The same thing happens when the sunlight shines through the rain.
Let's go to the waterfall and I'll show you.

Interesting!

The light from the sun shines through the water. The drops of water are like tiny prisms.

As the drops of water bend the light, we see the many colors of the rainbow.

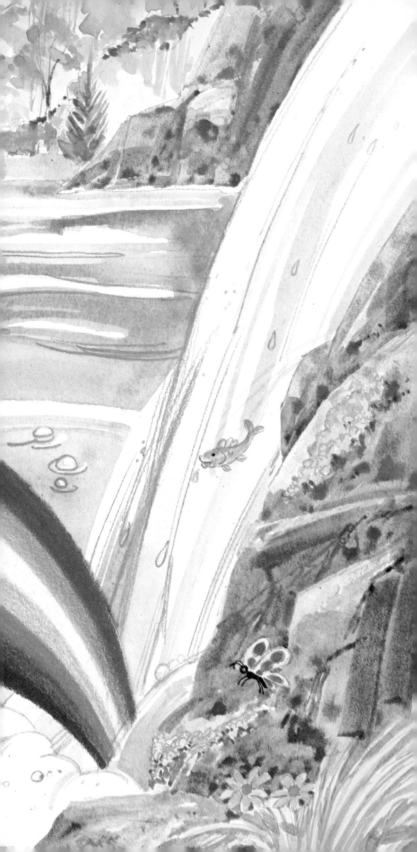

Let's go up into the sky
and look at the rainbow.

The sunlight shines
through the drops.
The raindrops are
like tiny prisms.
They bend the sunlight
and split it into many colors.

As we look
into the sky,
we see – –

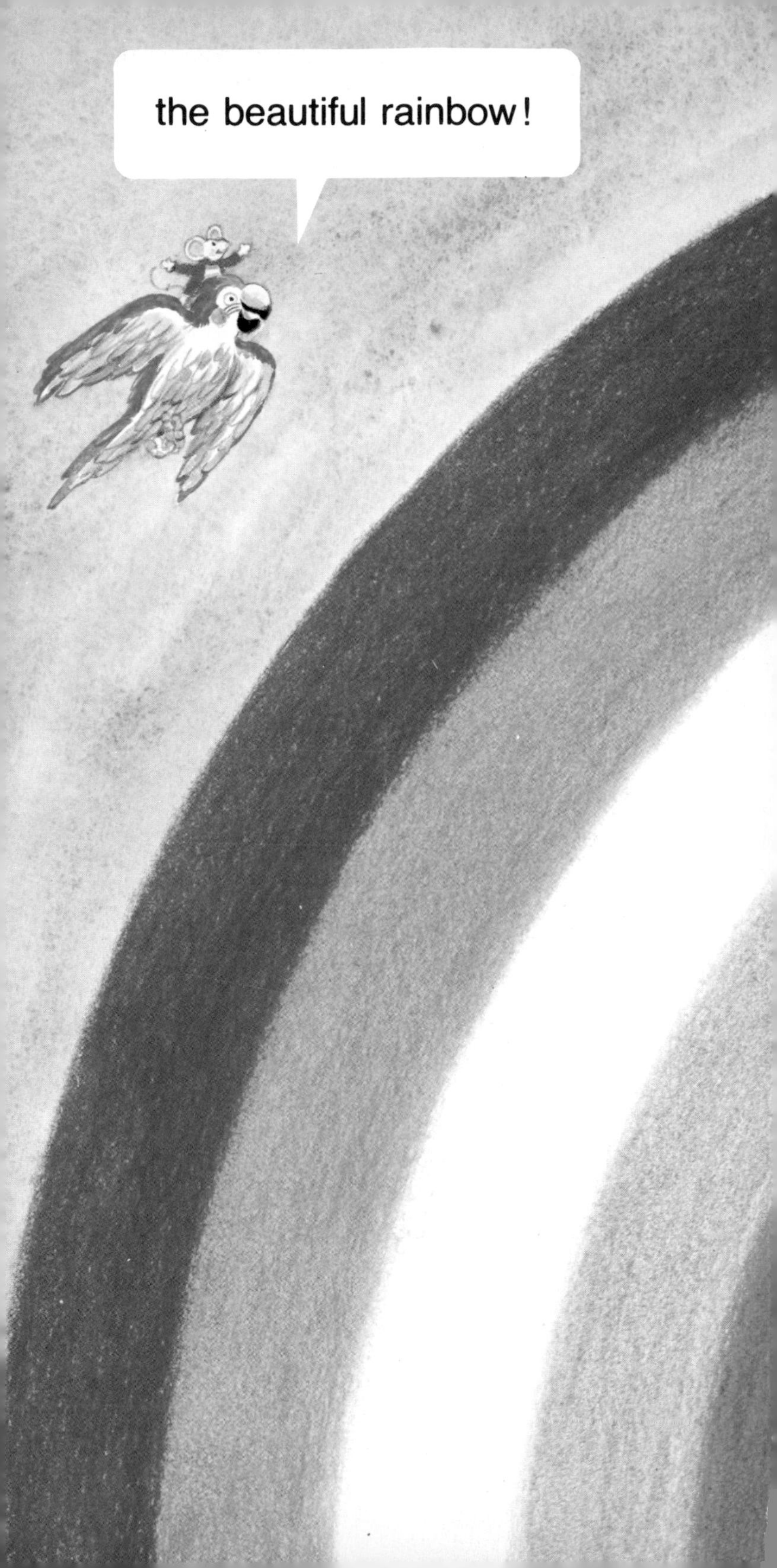
the beautiful rainbow!